D0912906

Big Cats

Jaguar

Written by
Lauren Diemer

www.av2books.com

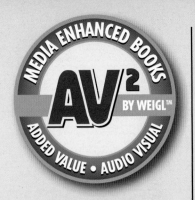

AV² provides enriched content that supplements and complements this book. Weigl's AV² books strive to create inspired learning and engage young minds in a total learning experience.

Your AV² Media Enhanced books come alive with...

Audio
Listen to sections of the book read aloud.

Key Words
Study vocabulary, and complete a matching word activity.

Video
Watch informative video clips.

Quizzes
Test your knowledge.

Go to **www.av2books.com**, and enter this book's unique code.

Embedded Weblinks
Gain additional information for research.

Slide Show
View images and captions, and prepare a presentation.

BOOK CODE

C491828

Try This!
Complete activities and hands-on experiments.

... and much, much more!

AV² by Weigl brings you media enhanced books that support active learning.

Published by AV² by Weigl
350 5th Avenue, 59th Floor
New York, NY 10118
Websites: www.av2books.com   www.weigl.com

Library of Congress Cataloging-in-Publication Data

Diemer, Lauren.
 Jaguar / Lauren Diemer.
    pages cm. -- (Big cats)
 Includes index.
 ISBN 978-1-4896-0918-2 (hardcover : alk. paper) -- ISBN 978-1-4896-0919-9 (softcover : alk. paper) --
ISBN 978-1-4896-0920-5 (single user ebk.) -- ISBN 978-1-4896-0921-2 (multi user ebk.)
1. Jaguar--Juvenile literature. I. Title.
 QL737.C23D54 2014
 599.75'5--dc 3

2014004620

Printed in the United States of America in North Mankato, Minnesota
1 2 3 4 5 6 7 8 9 0 18 17 16 15 14

032014
WEP150314

Editor Heather Kissock   Design Terry Paulhus

Contents

Meet the
Jaguar

Jaguars are the third-largest cat species in the world. Only the lion and tiger are larger. Jaguars are **predators** that hunt other animals for food. They have strong, stocky bodies to help them pounce on their **prey**. Jaguars prey on 85 **species** of animals.

The jaguar is the largest cat in North and South America. Jaguars once lived throughout the American continents. Now, they are found in only a few areas. Jaguars are solitary animals. This means they prefer to live alone.

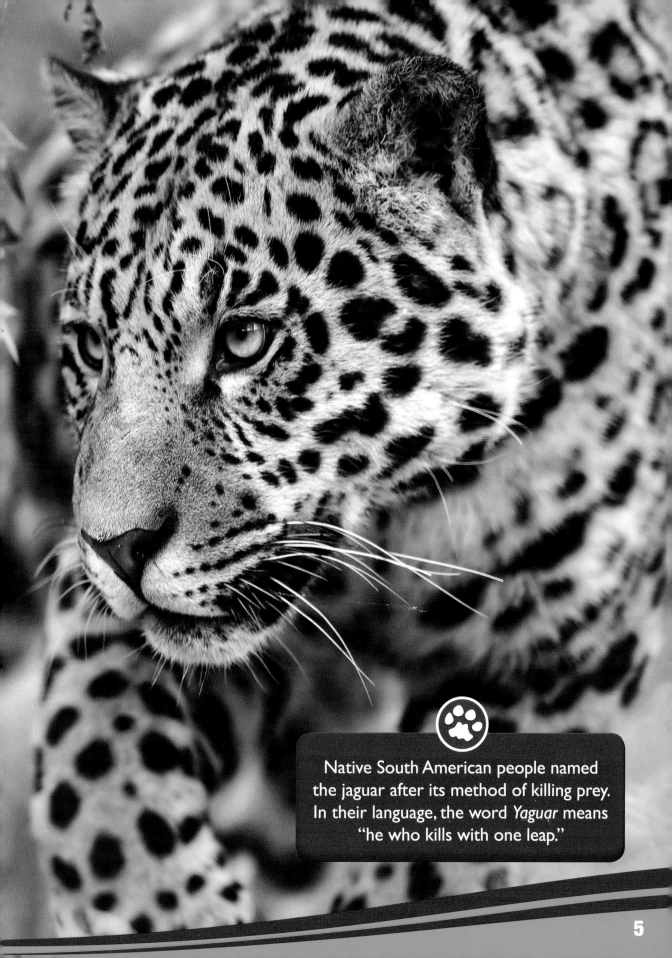

Native South American people named the jaguar after its method of killing prey. In their language, the word *Yaguar* means "he who kills with one leap."

All About
Jaguars

All cats belong to the group of animals called *felidae*. This **mammal** group includes house cats as well as big cats, such as jaguars, lions, and tigers. The jaguar's scientific name is *Panthera onca*.

Today, jaguars live mostly in South and Central America. The highest numbers of jaguars are found in South America's Amazon rainforest. The different types of jaguars are named after the areas in which they live. The Amazon, Panamanian, Peruvian, and Yucatan jaguars are all named based on their location.

The jaguar's fur varies from yellow to black and white to brown. The fur is covered with spots called rosettes.

Comparing Big Cats

The jaguar is often mistaken for the leopard. The two animals look similar but have unique features. The jaguar has spots inside the rosettes on its coat. The leopard does not. The jaguar has a stocky build, with shorter legs and a shorter tail than the leopard.

Jaguar

+ **Length:**
7–9 feet
(213–274 centimeters)
including tail
+ **Weight:**
100–250 pounds
(45–113 kilograms)
+ **Speed:**
Up to 40 miles per hour
(64 kilometers
per hour)

Lion

+ **Length:**
6.5–9 feet
(198–274 cm)
including tail
+ **Weight:**
265–420 lbs
(120–190 kg)
+ **Speed:**
Up to 35 mph (56 kph)

Tiger

+ **Length:**
7.5– 10.8 feet
(260–330 cm)
including tail
+ **Weight:**
220–675 pounds
(100–306 kg)
+ **Speed:**
Up to 40 miles per hour
(64 kph)

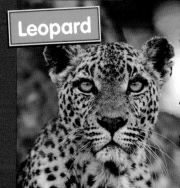

Leopard

+ **Length:**
6.5–9 feet
(198–274 cm)
including tail
+ **Weight:**
66–176 lbs (30–80 kg)
+ **Speed:**
Up to 57 mph (92 kph)

Cheetah

+ **Length:**
6–7 feet
(183– 213 cm)
including tail
+ **Weight:**
77–143 lbs (35– 65 kg)
+ **Speed:**
Up to 70 mph
(112 kph)

Cougar

+ **Length:**
5–9 feet
(152–274 cm)
including tail
+ **Weight:**
Up to 150 lbs (68 kg)
+ **Speed:**
Up to 35 mph (56 kph)

Jaguar History

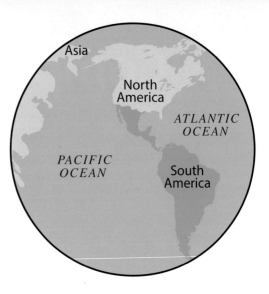

Asia

North America

ATLANTIC OCEAN

PACIFIC OCEAN

South America

Scientists believe that jaguars originated in Eurasia. They evolved from an **ancestor** of the leopard that lived more than 1.5 million years ago. The cat arrived in the Americas by crossing the **Bering Land Bridge**.

The early jaguars had longer legs than jaguars of today. It is believed that the legs became shorter as the jaguar **adapted** to its new environment.

Jaguars once lived throughout the southern United States and Mexico. Some groups of these cats, including the Arizona jaguar, have almost completely disappeared. Jaguars were also once common in Mexico. Today, it is estimated that Mexico has fewer than 900 jaguars. About 15,000 are left worldwide.

PREHISTORIC JAGUAR

Scientists have collected **fossil** remains of the jaguar in Tennessee, Texas, Missouri, and the La Brea Tar Pits in California.

Over the years, jaguars have lost more than 40 percent of their historical range. Now, they are found mainly in Latin America.

Where Jaguars Live

Jaguars live in large **territories.** These areas can be as large as 102 square miles (265 square kilometers). The male's territory can include the territories of several females. Jaguars mark their territory by spreading waste and clawing trees.

The jaguar lives in a variety of **habitats**. These habitats include forests, rainforests, swamps, and grasslands. The jaguar is able to hide among the plants in these regions. This helps it hunt and maintain its solitary life. Jaguar habitats stretch from Argentina in South America to the Grand Canyon in Arizona. Jaguars are now an **endangered** species in most of these habitats.

While jaguars can climb trees, they spend most of their time on the ground.

The jaguar is protected in nearly all the countries in which it lives.

Jaguar Features

Jaguars have bodies that make them strong hunters. They attack their prey quickly by pouncing with their short, powerful legs. Jaguars have sharp teeth and strong jaws to kill their prey. Excellent night vision helps them see in the dark and judge distance for stalking their prey. They sneak up on quiet, padded paws to make the kill.

Getting Closer

① Head

- Large head with room for strong jaw muscles
- Sharp teeth to bite prey

② Coat

- Can have different coloring
- White throat and underbelly
- Rosettes for markings

③ Eyes

- Reflect light to see better at night
- Can judge distances well to stalk prey

④ Legs

- Short legs, powerful muscles
- Help stalk and pounce on prey

⑤ Paws

- Padded for protection and quiet hunting
- Walks on toes to keep quiet

What Do Jaguars Eat?

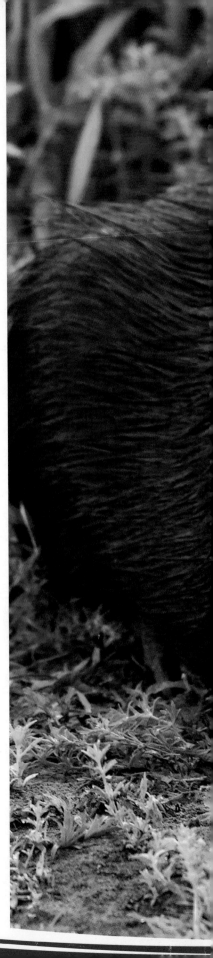

Jaguars hunt at any time of day. Their keen eyesight allows them to hunt under cover of darkness. Most often, they hunt at dawn and dusk. With their good **camouflage**, jaguars can hide easily from their prey. Moving through the dense plant growth, they slowly stalk their prey. When they are close enough, they pounce. Once the prey is caught, the jaguar kills it with one bite to the skull.

Most of a jaguar's hunting is done on land, where it preys on deer, monkeys, and other land animals. However, jaguars also hunt in the water. Frogs, fish, turtles, and **caimans** are just some of the water-based animals they hunt.

The capybara is another land animal jaguars hunt.

FOOD FIGHT

Jaguars are the top predators in the food chain and do not fear other animals or need to protect their prey from them.

Jaguar
Life Cycle

A jaguar's territory can cover a wide area. Finding a mate in such a large space can be a challenge. Females release a scent to let males know they are ready to mate. This is the only time male and females stay with each other. After mating, the males go back to their solitary lives. The females raise the cubs on their own.

Birth to 2 Weeks

Three months after mating, the mothers are ready to have their cubs. Mother jaguars give birth to litters of one to four babies. The cubs weigh about 2 pounds (0.9 kilograms) each. The babies will not open their eyes for two weeks. They are completely dependent on their mother.

Raising the cubs all by herself means that the female is in charge of their protection. When the mother is about to give birth, she finds a cave or other well-hidden spot for a **den**. Although the mother jaguar has no predators, the cubs are defenseless. The cubs remain in the den for about six months. The den helps to hide them from predators.

2 Years and Older

At about 2 years of age, jaguars are ready to leave their mothers and find their own territories. Males may stay in small groups at first before going off on their own. Females do not stray too far from their mother's territory. At about two years of age, females are ready to have cubs of their own. Jaguars in nature live for 11 to 15 years.

2 Weeks to 2 Years

The cubs drink milk from their mother for three to five months. They begin to eat meat at about 2 weeks of age. Their mother swallows the food and brings it back up for them until they are ready to eat solid food. By 6 months of age, the cubs are learning how to hunt.

Conservation of Jaguars

Jaguars are an endangered species that need help from humans to survive. Humans, however, are one of the jaguar's greatest threats. Many cattle ranchers feel that they have to kill jaguars to defend their livestock and property. In 1999, the Wildlife Conservation Society began a jaguar **conservation** program that works with cattle owners to stop them from killing the jaguars. The society has gained cooperation from governments in Central and South America to develop areas in which jaguars can travel safely.

Another threat to the jaguar is the loss of its habitat. Humans damage forests and grasslands. Cutting down trees for farms, homes, and cities means that the jaguar has less space to hunt and to hide. To remain safe from **extinction**, the jaguar needs protected lands.

ILLEGAL COATS

People once hunted jaguars for their beautiful coats. It is now against the law to hunt these endangered animals for their skins.

The government of Belize and the World Wildlife Fund (WWF) established 150 square miles (388.5 sq. km) of protected land for jaguars. About 200 jaguars live in the rainforest at the Cockscomb Basin Wildlife Sanctuary.

Myths and Legends

The jaguar has played an important role in the lives of many North and South American peoples. The Mayan, Aztec, and Inca peoples built temples to the jaguar. They believed that the jaguar held great power. One ancient Mexican group, the Olmec, worshiped jaguars as gods. Many of these groups believed that the jaguar had magical powers. The people wore jaguar clothing and jewelry so that they would have these powers as well.

American Indians also have had a strong connection to the jaguar. Rock paintings of jaguars have been found in Arizona, New Mexico, and Texas. Here, the jaguar was considered a symbol of the hunt. It provided hunters with the power needed to overcome their prey.

Meso-American people often built temples dedicated to the worship of jaguars.

Jaguar Food Chain

Think about the animals the jaguar relies on for food. What do these animals eat? Draw a food chain to show the flow of energy, or food, to the jaguar. Note that most food chains begin with the Sun.

Materials Needed: You will need access to a library or the internet, paper, and a pen or pencil.

STEP 1 Draw a circle on the right side of your paper, and write the word "Jaguar" inside.

STEP 2 Use the internet, your school library, and this book to find information about the jaguar's diet. Determine which animals the jaguar eats. Place the name of one of these animals in a circle to the left of the jaguar. Draw an arrow showing the direction the energy transfers.

STEP 3 Return to the internet and library, and find information about what this prey animal eats. Place this food on the chart to the left of the prey animal.

STEP 4 Continue researching until your food chain goes back the Sun. How important is the Sun to this food chain?

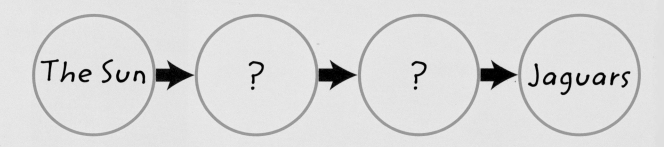

The Sun → ? → ? → Jaguars

5 Know Your FACTS

Test your knowledge of jaguars.

1 How much can a male jaguar weigh?

2 Where do jaguars live?

3 How many species of animal does the jaguar prey on?

4 At what age are jaguar cubs ready to leave their mother?

5 What other big cat is a jaguar often mistaken for?

Key Words

adapted: became better able to live in a particular place

ancestor: a person, plant, animal, or object from a past time

Bering Land Bridge: a long, thin stretch of land that once connected Alaska and Siberia

caimans: animals that live in South and Central America, similar to alligators

camouflage: the patterns and colors on an animal that allow it to blend into its surroundings

conservation: the protection of animals

den: the home of some kinds of animals

endangered: at risk of becoming extinct

extinction: when an animal species has completely died out

fossil: the remains of a living thing, such as a footprint or bone, from a previous time period

habitats: places where an animal lives naturally

mammal: an animal with fur that gives birth to live young

predators: animals that hunt other animals as food

prey: an animal hunted for food by another animal

species: animals or plants that share certain features and can breed together

territories: areas of land

Index

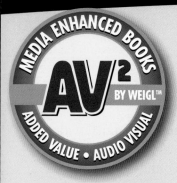

Log on to www.av2books.com

AV² by Weigl brings you media enhanced books that support active learning. Go to www.av2books.com, and enter the special code found on page 2 of this book. You will gain access to enriched and enhanced content that supplements and complements this book. Content includes video, audio, weblinks, quizzes, a slide show, and activities.

AV² Online Navigation

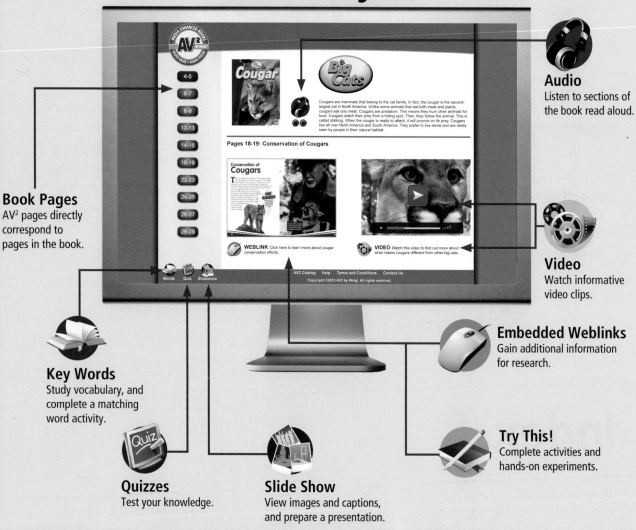

Book Pages
AV² pages directly correspond to pages in the book.

Audio
Listen to sections of the book read aloud.

Video
Watch informative video clips.

Embedded Weblinks
Gain additional information for research.

Key Words
Study vocabulary, and complete a matching word activity.

Try This!
Complete activities and hands-on experiments.

Quizzes
Test your knowledge.

Slide Show
View images and captions, and prepare a presentation.

AV² was built to bridge the gap between print and digital. We encourage you to tell us what you like and what you want to see in the future.

Sign up to be an AV² Ambassador at www.av2books.com/ambassador.